Ben has a spider.

Tessa screams.

"You rat!" says Tessa.
"Chicken!" says Ben.

"Stop it!" says Mum.
"Go to your room."

Ben gets a letter.

Tessa gets a letter.

Ben gets lots of letters.

Tessa gets lots of letters.

But then ...

I said stop it, Ben.

From,

Mum

Mum gets a letter.

"This is a better letter!" says Mum.